The Story of Hoover Dam

Gail Blasser Riley

Contents

Rigby®

A Harcourt Achieve Imprint

www.Rigby.com
1-800-531-5015

CHAPTER 1

The Need for a Dam

From Desert to Valley

Dry, cracked land stretched across southeastern California. Warm sun baked the land. Temperatures were perfect for farming, but there wasn't enough rainfall for crops. Nearby, the Colorado River raced through the Grand Canyon. How could people bring the river water to the dry land?

In 1901 workers decided to change the desert land
into farmland. They built dams made of dirt across
the river. The dams sent the river water into **irrigation**
ditches that had been cut into the desert floor.
Farmers were then able to grow grapes, lettuce, and
strawberries. This dry desert region became known as
the Imperial Valley.

The Imperial Valley

Flood!

In 1905 water from melting snow and heavy spring rains in the Rocky Mountains flowed into streams. The mountain streams carried the water to the Colorado River. The water washed away the small earth dams. From the river, the water raced into the irrigation ditches. The ditches overflowed and water poured into the valley. The floodwaters destroyed the rich farmland in the valley and the homes that were there.

THE FLOOD OF 1905

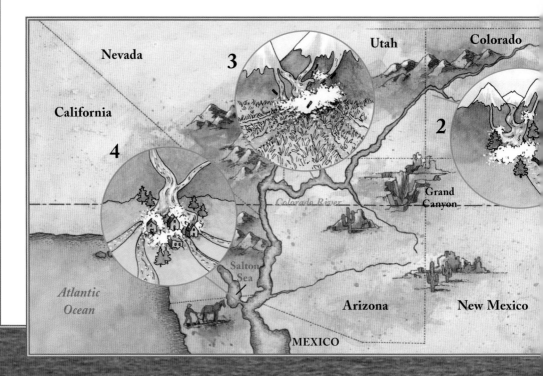

Nevada

3

Utah

Colorado

California

2

4

Grand Canyon

Colorado River

Salton Sea

Atlantic Ocean

Arizona

New Mexico

MEXICO

The farmers and townspeople hoped to return to their homes in the valley, but first they needed a way to control the river's flow. They couldn't afford another flood to wipe them out. They knew they would need something stronger than a dirt dam. They would need a huge dam to hold back the roaring waters of the Colorado River!

The Flood of 1905 created the Salton Sea in southeastern California.

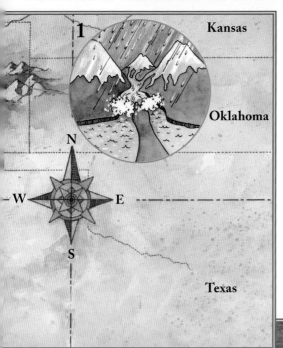

1. Rain falls and snow melts in Rocky Mountains.

2. Water fills mountain streams and the Colorado River.

3. Water races into irrigation ditches.

4. Water floods the land.

CHAPTER 2
Finding a Location

Grand Canyon

Colorado River

Dry and Lonely

How would people hold back the roaring river? After all, the Colorado River had been powerful enough to carve out a route through the Grand Canyon. It flowed so fast that hardly anyone tried to sail through its **currents**. Plus, the powerful river by itself wasn't the only problem. The river's route took it through the Southwest, the driest region in the United States.

Because of the heat and dry land, there weren't many towns near the river. There were no roads near most of the river, and there wasn't any electricity in the area. How hard would it be to build a large, strong dam? What kinds of materials would be needed? How would materials be delivered to the region? Could people work in the hot **climate**?

There weren't many towns in the hot, dry area around the Colorado River.

A Place to Build

President Theodore Roosevelt signed the National Reclamation Act. This law allowed the government to give money to projects that found ways to irrigate, or bring water to, dry desert lands. The U.S. government searched for the best place along the river to build a dam. A government report suggested that a high, **concrete** dam should be built on the Colorado River at or near Boulder Canyon on the Arizona and Nevada border. The location was later moved to Black Canyon. The dam, along with a **canal**, would control the Colorado River and bring water to the Imperial Valley. Construction was set to begin in 1931.

President Theodore Roosevelt

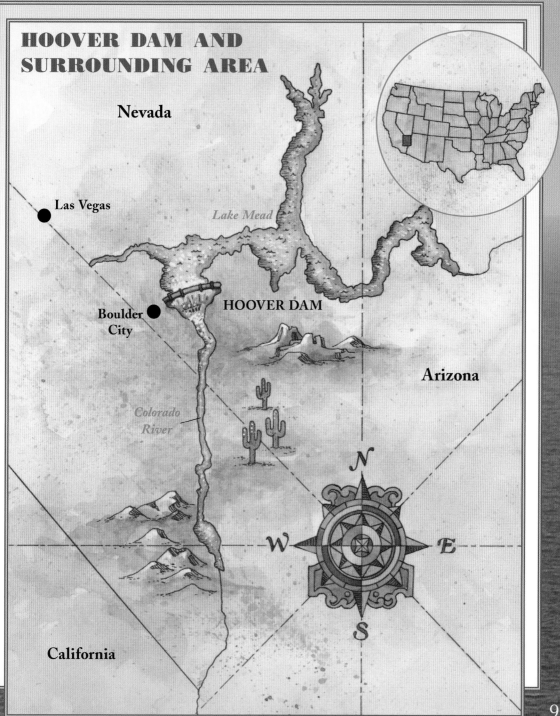

HOOVER DAM AND SURROUNDING AREA

Nevada

Las Vegas

Lake Mead

HOOVER DAM

Boulder City

Arizona

Colorado River

California

N

W

E

S

Preparing to Build

Much work needed to be done before the building of the dam could begin. Boulder City was built near the canyon so the builders of the dam would have a place to live. Houses and dining halls gave workers places to sleep and eat. A road was built from Boulder City to where the dam would be built. Workers also laid almost thirty-three miles of new railroad track from Las Vegas to the dam's location. A new power line that was almost 222 miles long was built to bring electricity to the area.

A town was built for the dam builders to live in.

CHAPTER 3
Building the Dam

Building Tunnels

Before construction could begin, the builders of the dam needed a way to keep the building location dry and safe from flooding. They decided to move the river! To do this, they drilled tunnels through the canyon walls. Then the river was **rerouted** through the tunnels.

Workers drilled four tunnels. Each tunnel measured 56 feet across and could carry more than 1.5 million gallons of water per second. The tunnels had concrete linings that were three feet thick. Together, the tunnels ran for more than three miles.

Workers drilled large tunnels.

Rough Working Conditions

Building the dam was hard work. The desert conditions made it even more challenging. In the summer, temperatures were often higher than 120 degrees Fahrenheit. Dust filled workers' mouths and noses. In the winter, temperatures dropped below freezing. The climate conditions put the workers' health at risk.

Workers needed to be aware of what was happening around them as they did their jobs. **Dynamite** blasts caused rock slides. Falling rock could seriously hurt or even kill a worker.

Big companies wanted the dam completed very quickly. Some said that the need to work quickly became more important than the need to work safely. However, workers didn't complain because they were happy to have jobs.

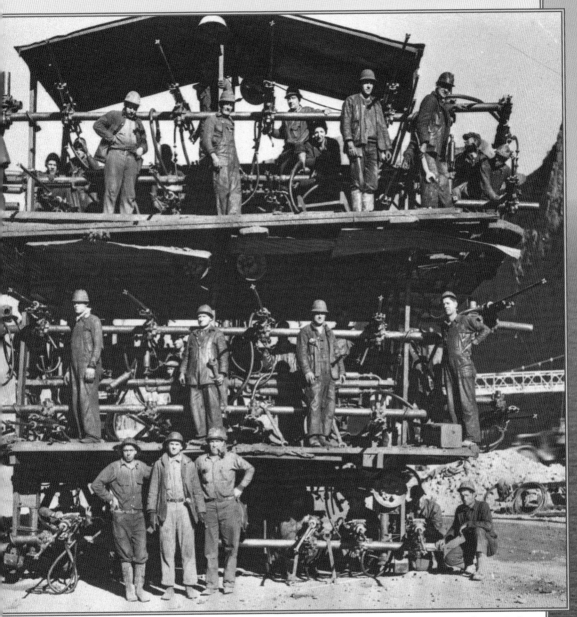

Workers were very happy to have jobs.

High Scalers

One of the hardest jobs was the role of high scaler. High scalers were needed because canyon walls had been worn away by millions of years of weather and climate changes. Water had frozen in cracks in the canyon walls. The ice in the cracks had split the rocks and loosened them. It was the job of high scalers to remove the loose rocks. They drilled holes with jackhammers and packed dynamite into holes.

High scalers worked
to remove loose rock.

A High Scaler's Job

Imagine pushing off on a rope down the side of a canyon. Tools, dynamite sticks, and water bags hang from your belt and weigh you down as you try to move across the canyon wall. Workers high above you lower a forty-four pound jackhammer to you. You must grip your rope and make your way down the wall as you reach for the jackhammer. Keeping an eye out for falling rocks and dropped tools that could hit you on the head can mean the difference between life and death.

Adding Spillways

The plans for building the dam required spillways. Spillways would be used when the Colorado River flooded. Before rising river water could reach the top of the dam, the spillways would drain the water into special tunnels. This would keep the river water from flowing over the top of the dam and flooding the land. The tunnels would route the water away from the river and into a lake behind the dam.

Spillways kept water from reaching the top of the dam.

The building plans also called for four towers. Two towers would be built on each side of the dam. These towers would collect water and send it to a power plant that was built at the base of the dam.

A federal highway was constructed across the top of the dam. It would be the shortest way to get from Las Vegas, Nevada to places on the East Coast.

A highway was built on top of the dam.

Construction Is Completed

In February, 1935 the last bit of concrete was poured. The tunnels that had been built to reroute the river were plugged. After the tunnels were plugged, the mighty waters of the Colorado River began to back up behind the dam. The rising water formed Lake Mead. The Colorado River was finally under control!

In 1947 Herbert Hoover was the president of the United States, so the U.S. government officially named the dam Hoover Dam. When it was completed, Hoover Dam was the tallest dam on the planet. It stood more than 700 feet above the Colorado River.

Hoover Dam Facts

- The dam was officially completed in 1936.
- The final cost of construction was $165 million.
- Workers finished the dam ahead of schedule.
- The dam weighs more than 6,600,000 tons.
- Workers used enough concrete in the dam to build a four-foot-wide sidewalk around the earth.
- Supplies and materials for the dam came from every state in the United States.
- About 20,000 vehicles a day use the highway on the top of the dam to travel between Nevada and Arizona.

CHAPTER 4
Hoover Dam Today

The Power of Water

Hoover Dam does what it was designed to do. It controls the powerful waters of the Colorado River, directing the river's flow to bring water and electricity to the region. The power plant at Hoover Dam makes enough electricity in one day to keep 500,000 homes for a whole year!

Thousands of people travel each year to see Hoover Dam. They also enjoy boating and swimming in Lake Mead, which is the largest man-make lake in the United States. What was once an empty desert is now filled with people and towns. Who knew 6.6 tons of concrete could change so much!

Glossary

canal a waterway made by digging

climate the weather in a place

concrete a mixture of sand, gravel, and cement that hardens when it dries

currents paths of water

dynamite a powerful explosive used to blow things up

irrigation system of supplying land with water through canals, pipes, and ditches

rerouted sent in a different direction

Index